MW01380809

Water Bath Canning and Preserving Cookbook For Beginners

Master Your Canning Preserving Skills, 1000 Days of Tasty Recipes to Learn How to Can Meat, Vegetable and Much More

by

Courtney May

TABLE OF CONTENT

CHAPTER 1: INTRODUCTION

Food preservation has evolved significantly in the 180 years since it was first used to store food. Canning and other forms of preservation is a technique used in food handling to avoid spoilage.

The first section of this cookbook discusses canning and preserving food methods, canning equipment, benefits of canning, some tips to get started as well as how to properly use jars and lids.

The second section of this book contains simple and delicious canning recipes for jams, jellies, butters, fruits, vegetables, meats, pickles, and relishes. Each set of instructions includes helpful guidelines for selecting the appropriate quantities and quality of raw foods.

The art of Food Preservation

Food preservation is often passed down through generations as a way to reconnect with simpler times. Furthermore, it can be done as a family activity and used as a teaching tool about the origins of food.

Food has always been preserved by humans. Our ancestors used it to get through the leaner, more insecure times and utilize any surplus out of necessity.

The sun became very important and with time, curing, smoking, and food dehydrators were invented. Ice-houses evolved into fridge-freezers. And canning has remained largely unchanged in practice. Not to mention other favorite methods, sugaring and pickling.

Methods for the preservation of food

Here is a list of preservation methods that have been in use since time immemorial:

A. Drying

This method lowers water activity, preventing bacterial growth. Drying can be done naturally using sun and wind. In modern times, it is achieved by use of dryers, fluidized dryers, freeze dryers, shelf dryers, spray dryers, dehydrators, and ovens.

B. Freezing

Freezing is the process of storing prepared foods in cold storage.

C. Smoking

This is preservation by means of exposing food to smoke from burning wood.

D. Vacuum Packing

By making bags and bottles airtight, vacuum packing removes all oxygen and bacteria die.

E. Salting and Pickling

Curing/salting, removes moisture from foods while pickling refers to preserving food in brine or marinating in vinegar.

F. Using Sugar Syrup

Sugar syrup form or crystallized sugar can be used to preserve food.

G. Using Sodium hydroxide

Sodium hydroxide makes food alkaline and this prevents bacterial growth.

H. Canning and bottling

This is whereby cooked food is sealed under pressure or in hot so as to kill bacteria.

I. Jellying

This is preserving food by cooking it in a material that solidifies into a gel like jelly, marmalade, or fruit preserves and conserves.

J. Jugging

Jugging involves stewing meat with brine, wine or animal's blood in an earthenware jug.

K. Modified atmosphere

This method preserves food using an atmosphere that has been altered to reduce oxygen concentration and increase carbon dioxide concentration.

L. Controlled use of organism

This method is used on cheese, wine, and beer by introducing benign organisms into it, where they create an environment unsuitable for harmful pathogens to grow.

M. High pressure food preservation

This technique uses 70,000 pounds of pressure to press foods inside a vessel. This kills micro-organisms and prevents spoilage.

N. Pasteurisation and Irradiation

Energy is used in food irradiation and pasteurization to kill microbes. Pasteurization uses heat, whereas irradiation uses the energy of ionizing radiation.

Water Bath, Fermenting, Pickling & Oil Canning

A. Water Bath Canning

Water bath processing is whereby jars are filled with high acid food, sealed, and boiled vigorously in water. Tomatoes, berries, fruit, sauerkraut, and pickled vegetables, jams, jellies, and pickled vegetables can all be preserved using this method.

Water canning MUST not be used for low-acid vegetables, meats, seafood, poultry, chili and beans, corn, or other grains.

B. Fermenting Canning

This is a technique whereby enzymes and micro-organisms are stimulated to produce to produce adenosine triphosphate and subsequently release acid, alcohol, and gases during the fermentation process. Fermentation produces lactic acid, found in pickled cucumbers, kombucha, kimchi, yogurt, wine, beer and other sour products. These chemical changes in organic substrates is what preserves the food or drink.

C. Pickle Canning

Pickling is a technique that preserves vegetables by means of fermentation with a brine or vinegar:

- **Using a Vinegar Brine for Pickling-**Vinegar, water, and salt are combined and used in the water bath method.
- **Natural Fermentation Pickling**-Here, salt is used to draw out water and create a brine. This is mostly used to make sauerkraut.

D. In-oil Canning

Using water bath canning for products entirely submerged in oil is a bad idea. However, if the product has plenty of acid and a small amount of oil, it's fine to can it. The only thing you have to do is to wipe the jar rims properly using white vinegar on your wiping cloth.

Preparation plan

E. Inspect food preservation equipment and food dehydrators before the start of the canning season.
F. Purchase the best canning jars and lids for use during the season. Jars should not have any nicks or scratches.
G. Check the accuracy of the pressure canners.
H. Always use a tried-and-true recipe from a reputable source.

Benefits of Home Canning

A. You get to eat real food

Home-canned goods are more nutritious and have much more health benefits.

B. You can Ditch salt and sugar

Don't like sugar or salt? With canning, you can decide to go salt-free or sugar-free!

C. Better diet

Canned goods are high in vitamins, minerals, and other nutrients that your body requires to thrive. They're also low in cholesterol, fat and calories.

D. Protecting planet earth

Canning minimizes food and packaging waste. This is especially true for home-grown food, which does not require long-distance transportation from farm to factory to distributor to supermarket.

E. Cheaper in the Long Haul

You get to buy ingredients in bulk, meaning cheaper prices and second-hand supplies. Canning will save you money if you stick with it.

F. Support local farmers

Local growers value the canning business because it helps them stay profitable, particularly smaller operations. This, in turn, stimulates the local economy.

What you need to get started

To begin preserving food at home, you will need the following items:

Food thermometer

Temperature, seal, and timing are all important factors in preventing dangerous bacteria and botulism toxins from growing in your preserved foods. A food thermometer is required for safe canning and storing.

Lemon Juice or Citric Acid

Organic lemon juice is an additive that helps increase acidity and make your canning method safer.

Canning/Pickling Salt

Canning and Pickling Salt lacks iodine and anti-caking chemicals found in table salt. These chemicals can also affect the flavor and color of canned products.

Pressure Canner

This kills all bacteria when canning.

Other Requirements

- Jars and lids – in various sizes
- Jar lifter or canning tongs
- A stock pot

- Canning rack
- A ladle – for filling
- Wide-mouth funnel
- Timer

Tips for Food Safety

Food safety is essential when canning to reduce food-borne illnesses. Here how to ensure food safety:

A. Before adding your produce, always start with clean, sanitized jars.
B. Washing your produce with a fruit and vegetable scrubber will help to reduce germ spread.
C. When washing fruits and vegetables, avoid using any type of cleaning solution.
D. After cleaning your jars, store them in a clean area away from food and dirty items until you are ready to use them.
E. Avoid using old or unsafe recipes, as well as untested recipes or guidelines.
F. Use the proper jar size and avoid over-tightening the screw band.
G. Make sure to account for altitude and other factors.

Mistakes to avoid

Avoid the following common canning mistakes:

A. Using Pressure Canner instead of a Boiling Water Bath and vice-versa
B. Not adjusting Canning Time or altitude
C. Filling the Jars to Overflow
D. Reusing Canning Lids
E. Using Canning Jars that are cracked or chipped
F. Using inferior ingredients
G. Not allowing the jars to cool undisturbed

Preparation of jars and lid

Follow the steps below in this critical step of canning:

Check your canning jars
Look for any flaws, nicks, cracks, unevenness, and so on. This is an important step because flaws in your canning jars may cause the canning process to fail.

Clean the Jars:
If there are no flaws, wash your canning jars in hot, soapy water and properly rinse them.

Heat your canning jars:
Preheat jars in a pan with water; heat to about 180 degrees.

Lids and bands:
Select the right size lids and bands for the jars you'll be using and examine them for flaws and damage. Rinse lids and bands in hot, soapy water after washing.
Preheat lids before using; this helps the lids to seal properly.

Choosing the best fruits and vegetables to Can

A. Berries and fruits
Most fruits and berries are good for canning because of their high acidity level. Check the quality of texture and firmness. Apples, pears, peaches, plums, nectarines, strawberries and blueberries best fruits for canning.

B. Tomatoes and Tomato-Related Products
Tomatoes are ideal for simple water-bath canning because they have a relatively high acidity level. Add lemon juice/citric acid to help with food safety.

C. Most vegetables, including corn, green beans, and squash
Corn, green beans, carrots, squash, and most vegetables are great for pressure canning.

How to prepare vegetable and fruit preserves

Different foods necessitate different preparation methods. Here are the preparation and equipment instructions:

1. **Cleaning**

- **Tomatoes**-Clean, remove stems and any bruises. Cut into quarters.
- **Asparagus-Clean** and trim asparagus spears.
- **Beets**-Trim and boil to remove the skins.
- **Carrots**-Wash, peel and dice.
- **Corn**-Cut the kernels from the cob.
- **Cucumbers**-Use them as they are or pickle them.
- **Green beans**-Can them raw.
- **Okra**-Wash, trim, and leave whole.
- **Peppers**-Blister peppers and then remove the skins.
- **Peaches**-Handle gently so they do not bruise.

B. Sterilisation
Jars must be sterilized before filling and processing.

C. Filling The Canning Jars
It is critical that the jars are properly filled with correct head-space, in order to produce a safe product when the processing is finished.

How can you recognize Botulism in jars

Clostridium botulinum bacteria is the most common producer of the toxin that causes botulism. To avoid botulism, take the following precautions:

- Always use proper canning techniques.
- If food was not canned properly, Discard.
- Throw out contaminated food.
- DO NOT taste food to check if it's safe.
- Discard if the container looks damaged.
- Discard if the container leaks foam.
- Discard if the food is moldy.
- Discard if the container is leaking.
- Discard if the food is discolored.
- Discard if the container is smelly.

CHAPTER 2: SUGAR-FREE JAM

1. Sugar-Free raspberry lemonade jam

MAKES 6 250-ml JARS

Ingredients:

- 3½ lb. fresh raspberries, crashed
- ½ cup fresh lemon juice
- 4 Tablespoons No-Sugar Pectin
- 1½ cups honey

Directions:

1. Place raspberries in a Dutch oven.
2. Stir in lemon juice and pectin. Boil the mixture.
3. Stir in honey. Heat another 1 minute.
4. Fill into a hot jar, leaving ¼-inch of space. Release air bubbles and center the lid. Apply the band and make it snug.
5. Place jar in boiling-water canner.
6. Process for 10 minutes, accounting for altitude.
7. Remove jars and cool

2. Sugar-Free strawberry-tequila jam

MAKES 4 250-ml JARS

Ingredients:

- 5 cups chopped fresh strawberries, crushed
- ½ cup tequila
- 5 Tablespoons No-Sugar Pectin
- 1 cup agave syrup

Directions:

1. Combine strawberries and tequila in a Dutch oven.
2. Stir in pectin.
3. Boil the mixture.
4. Stir in agave syrup. Heat another 1 minute.
5. Fill into a hot jar, leaving ¼-inch of space. Release air bubbles and center the lid. Apply the band and make it snug. Put jar in canner with boiling water.
6. Process for 10 minutes, accounting for altitude.
7. Remove jars and cool.

CHAPTER 3: CHUTNEY

4. Cranberry orange chutney

Ingredients:

- 24 ounces whole cranberries, rinsed
- 2 cups white onion, chopped
- 4 teaspoons ginger , peeled, grated
- 2 cups golden raisin
- 1 1/2 cups white sugar
- 2 cups 5% white distilled vinegar
- 1 1/2 cups brown sugar
- 1 cup orange juice
- 3 sticks cinnamon

Directions:

1. Combine all Ingredients using a Dutch oven. Boil on high; simmer for 15 minutes.
2. Remove cinnamon sticks and discard.
3. Fill into jars, leaving 1/2-inch of space.
4. Release air bubbles.
5. Close the jars tightly, then heat for 5 minutes in a water bath.

---

4. Mango chutney

Ingredients:

- 11 cups chopped unripe mango
- 2 1/2 Tablespoons grated fresh ginger
- 4 1/2 cups sugar
- 1 teaspoon canning salt
- 1 1/2 Tablespoons chopped fresh garlic
- 3 cups 5% white distilled vinegar
- 2 1/2 cups yellow onion, chopped
- 2 1/2 cups golden raisins
- 4 teaspoons chili powder

Directions:

1. Combine sugar and vinegar in a stockpot. Bring 5 minutes. Add all other Ingredients.
2. Simmer 25 minutes, moving sporadically.
3. Fill mixture into jars, leaving 1/2-inch of space. Release air bubbles.
4. Close the jars tightly, then heat for 5 minutes in a water bath.

CHAPTER 4: JELLIES

5. Apple Jelly without Added Pectin

Ingredients:

- 4 cups apple juice
- 2 tablespoons strained lemon juice
- 3 cups sugar

Directions:

1. Combine apple juice, lemon juice and sugar in a kettle.
2. Boil on high to 8 °F above the boiling point of water.
3. Take off the heat; swiftly skim all foam off. Pour jelly into hot, sterile canning jars to ¼ inch from top.
4. Close the jars tightly, then heat for 5 minutes in a water bath.

5. Blackberry Jelly without Added Pectin

Ingredients:

- 8 cups blackberry juice, freshly squeezed
- 6 cups sugar

Directions:

1. Combine sugar and juice in a kettle.
2. Boil on high to above 8 °F.
3. Take off the heat; swiftly skim all foam off. Pour jelly into hot, sterile canning jars to ¼ inch from top.
4. Close the jars tight, then heat for five minutes in the water bath.

---

6. Cherry Jelly with pectin

Ingredients:

- 4 ½ cups sugar
- 3 ½ cups cherry juice, freshly squeezed
- 1 package pectin

Directions:

1. Combine juice and pectin in a kettle.
2. Heat to a full rolling boil.
3. Add sugar, continue stirring, and boil rapidly for 1 minute.
4. Take off the heat; swiftly skim all foam off. Pour jelly into hot, sterile canning jars, allowing ¼ inch of space.
5. Close the jars tight, then heat for five minutes in the water bath.

8. Cinnamon Orange Jelly

MAKES 4 HALF-PINT JARS

Ingredients:

- 2 cups orange juice
- 2/3 cup water
- 4 sticks cinnamon
- 1 package pectin
- 2 tablespoons orange peel, chopped
- 1/3 cup lemon juice
- 1 teaspoon whole allspice
- ½ teaspoon whole cloves
- 3 ½ cups sugar

Directions:

1. Mix orange juice, lemon juice, and water in a pan.
2. Stir in pectin.
3. Arrange orange peel, allspice, cloves, and cinnamon sticks in a cloth, tie with a string, and add fruit mixture.
4. Heat, stirring regularly, bring quickly to a rolling boil.
5. Add sugar, stir and boil rapidly for 1 minute.
6. Take off the heat. Remove spice bag and swiftly skim all foam off. Pour jelly into hot, sterile canning jars to ¼ inch from top.
7. Close the jars tight, then heat for five minutes in the water bath.

---

8. Grape-plum jelly

Ingredients:

- 3 1/2 lbs. ripe plums, ashed and pitted
- 3 lbs. ripe Concord grapes, washed
- 1/2 teaspoons butter
- 1 cup water
- 8-1/2 cups sugar
- 4 oz. pectin

Directions:

1. Crush the plums and grapes in a pan with water. Boil and then simmer for 10 minutes.
2. Strain juice through a cheesecloth.
3. Combine juice, butter and pectin; boil on high, stirring regularly.
4. Add the sugar and boil rapidly for 1 minute.
5. Take off the heat, remove foam, and fill sterile jars, leaving 1/4-inch of space.
6. Close the jars tightly, then heat for 5 minutes in a water bath.

10. Grape Juice Jelly with pectin

MAKES 8 OR 9 HALF-PINT JARS

Ingredients:

- 5 cups grape juice, fresh
- 7 cups sugar
- 1 package pectin

Directions:

1. Combine juice and pectin in a kettle.
2. Heat to a full rolling boil.
3. Add sugar, continue stirring, and boil rapidly for 1 minute.
4. Take off the heat; swiftly skim all foam off. Pour jelly into hot, sterile canning jars, allowing ¼ inch of space. Close the jars tightly, then heat for 5 minutes in a water bath.

---

11. Mixed Fruit Jelly with Liquid Pectin

MAKES NINE OR TEN 8-OUNCE JARS

Ingredients:

- 2 cups cranberry juice, freshly squeezed
- 2 cups quince juice, freshly squeezed
- 1 cup apple juice, freshly squeezed
- 7 ½ cups sugar
- ½ bottle liquid pectin

Directions:

1. Combine juices and sugar in a kettle.
2. Heat, stirring regularly, bring quickly to a rolling boil.
3. Add pectin and continue boiling for 1 minute.
4. Take off the heat; swiftly skim all foam off.
5. Pour jelly into hot jars, allowing ¼ inch of space.
6. Close the jars tight, then heat for five minutes in the water bath.

12. Mixed pepper jelly

Ingredients:

- 5 cups chopped yellow bell peppers, washed
- 5 cups sugar
- ½ cup chopped Serrano chile peppers, washed
- 1 1/2 cups 5% white distilled vinegar
- 3 oz. liquid pectin

Directions:

1. Place sweet and hot peppers in a blender.
2. Add vinegar and purée the peppers. Combine the pepper-vinegar purée and remaining vinegar into a big saucepan.
3. Heat for 10 minutes.
4. Take off the heat and strain using a jelly bag.
5. Add 2 1/4 cups of the pepper-vinegar juice back into the saucepan. Stir in sugar and return to a boil. Add the pectin, return to a full rolling boil rapidly for 1 minute, stirring regularly.
6. Take off the heat, remove any foam, and fill into sterile jars, leaving 1/4-inch of space.
7. Close the jars tightly, then heat for 5 minutes in a water bath.

---

13. Orange Lemonade Jelly

MAKES 5 half-pint jars

Ingredients:

- 3 ¼ cups sugar
- ½ bottle liquid pectin
- 1 cup water
- 3 tablespoons lemon juice
- 6-ounce can frozen concentrated orange juice

Directions:

1. Stir the sugar into the water. Heat, stirring regularly, bring quickly to a rolling boil.
2. Add lemon juice. boil rapidly for 1 minute.
3. Take off the heat. Stir in pectin. Add thawed concentrated orange juice and mix well.
4. Pour jelly into hot, sterile canning jars, allowing ¼ inch of space. Close the jars tightly, then heat for 5 minutes in a water bath.

14. Plum Jelly with Liquid Pectin

MAKES 7 OR 8 HALF-PINT JARS

Ingredients:

- 4 cups plum juice
- 7 ½ cups sugar
- ½ bottle liquid pectin

Directions:

1. Combine sugar and juice in a kettle.
2. Place on high heat and boil.
3. Add pectin; boil rapidly for 1 minute.
4. Take off the heat; swiftly skim all foam off. Pour jelly into hot, sterile canning jars, allowing ¼ inch of space. Close the jars tightly, then heat for 5 minutes in a water bath.

---

15. Quince Jelly without Added Pectin

MAKES FOUR 8-OUNCE JARS

Ingredients:

- 3 ¾ cups quince juice
- 1/3 cup lemon juice
- 3 cups sugar

Directions:

1. Combine quince juice, lemon juice and sugar in a kettle.
2. Boil on high to above 8 °F.
3. Take off the heat; swiftly skim all foam off. Pour jelly into hot, sterile canning jars, allowing ¼ inch of space.
4. Close the jars tight, then heat for five minutes in the water bath.

16. Strawberry-rhubarb jelly

Ingredients:

- 1 1/2 quarts' ripe strawberries, washed and diced
- 1/2 teaspoons butter
- 1 1/2 lbs. red stalks of rhubarb, washed and diced
- 6 cups sugar
- 6 oz. liquid pectin

Directions:

1. Place both fruits in a cheesecloth and extract juice.
2. Add 3 1/2 cups of juice into a pan.
3. Add butter and sugar, properly mixing into juice.
4. Boil on high, stirring regularly. Stir in pectin. Bring to a full rolling Heat another 1 minute.
5. Take off the heat, remove foam, and fill sterile jars, leaving 1/4-inch of space.
6. Close the jars tightly, then heat for 5 minutes in a water bath.

CHAPTER 5: PRESERVES AND CONSERVES

17. Apple-Cranberry Conserve

MAKES: 3-4 Half-Pint jars

Ingredients:

- 1 Granny Smith apple, peeled, cored, and diced
- 1 ½ cups fresh cranberries
- Zest and juice of 1 orange
- 1 ¾ cups sugar
- ¾ cup chopped walnuts or pecans
- Zest and juice of 1 lemon
- ¾ cup raisins
- 1 cup water

Directions:

1. Using a shallow saucepan, combine the water, cranberries, and sugar.
2. Boil the mixture and simmer for 5 minutes, stirring continuously.
3. Mix in the juice, zest, and apple.
4. Boil the mixture to 220°F; cook for about 15 minutes over medium heat. Keep stirring periodically
5. Mix in the nuts and raisins.
6. Transfer into pre-sterilized jars using a jar funnel. Allow a space of ¼ inch.
7. Then, close the jars. Adjust the bands to seal and prevent any leakage.

18. Cantaloupe Peach Conserve

MAKES: 3 Half-Pint jars

Ingredients:

- ¼ cup blanched almonds, coarsely chopped
- 1 ½ cups cantaloupe, chopped
- 1 ½ cups peaches, peeled and chopped
- 2 cups sugar
- ½ tablespoon lemon juice
- ¼ teaspoon ground nutmeg
- 1/8 teaspoon salt
- 1/8 teaspoon grated orange rind

Directions:

1. Using a shallow saucepan, combine the cantaloupe and peaches.
2. Boil for about 10 minutes. Keep stirring periodically.
3. Stir in sugar and lemon juice.
4. Mix in the remaining ingredients.
5. Boil the mixture to 220°F; cook for about 10-12 minutes over medium heat. Keep stirring periodically
6. Transfer into pre-sterilized jars using a jar funnel. Allow a space of ¼ inch.
7. Then, close the jars. Adjust the bands to seal and prevent any leakage.
8. Heat in a water bath for 15 minutes.

---

19. Ginger-Pear Preserve

MAKES: 3-4 Half-Pint jars

Ingredients:

- 4 cups pears. Peeled, seeded, and chopped
- ½ teaspoon salt
- 2 ½ cups honey
- 1 lemon, peeled and diced

Directions:

1. Using a shallow saucepan, combine the ingredients.
2. Boil the mixture to 220°F; cook for about 12-15 minutes over medium heat. Keep stirring periodically
3. Transfer into pre-sterilized jars using a jar funnel. Allow a space of ¼ inch.
4. Then, close the jars.
5. Adjust the bands to seal and prevent any leakage.

20. Peach-Lemon Preserve

MAKES: 4 Half-Pint jars

Ingredients:

- Juice of 2 lemons
- 3 pounds peaches, peeled, pitted, and cubed
- 1 ½ cups granulated sugar

Directions:

1. Using a shallow saucepan, combine the peaches, lemon juice and sugar.
2. Set the mixture aside for 2-4 hours.
3. Boil the mixture to 220°F; cook for about 1-2 hours over medium heat. Keep stirring periodically
4. Transfer into pre-sterilized jars using a jar funnel. Allow a space of ¼ inch.
5. Then, close the jars. Adjust the bands to seal and prevent any leakage.
6. Process jars in a water bath for about 10 minutes

---

21. Spiced Apple-Lemon Preserve

MAKES: 3 Half-Pint jars

Ingredients:

- 3 cups apples, peeled, cored and sliced
- ½ cup water
- 1 teaspoon ground nutmeg
- 1.75-ounce pectin
- ½ tablespoon lemon juice
- 1 lemon, unpeeled, seeded, and sliced
- 2 cups sugar

Directions:

1. Using a shallow saucepan, combine the water, sugar, lemon juice, lemon slices, and apples.
2. Boil for about 8-10 minutes over medium heat. Keep stirring periodically.
3. Mix in the pectin and nutmeg.
4. Boil the mixture to 220°F; cook over medium heat. Keep stirring periodically.
5. Transfer into pre-sterilized jars using a jar funnel. Allow a space of ¼ inch.
6. Then, close the jars. Adjust the bands to seal and prevent any leakage.
7. Process jars in a water bath for about 10 minutes

22. Watermelon Lemon Preserves

MAKES: 4 Half-Pint Jars

Ingredients:

- 3 cups white sugar
- 2 lbs. watermelon, peeled, seeded and cubed
- 3 lemons unpeeled, sliced, and seeded

Directions:

1. In a cooking pot, combine the watermelon cubes, lemons and sugar.
2. Boil for about 2 hours over medium heat until fir and thick. Keep stirring periodically.
3. Transfer into pre-sterilized jars using a jar funnel. Allow a space of ¼ inch.
4. Then, close the jars. Adjust the bands to seal and prevent any leakage.

CHAPTER 6: BUTTERS

23. Apple butter

Ingredients:

- 2 cups cider
- 8 lbs. Apples, washed, quartered, and cored
- 2 Tablespoons cinnamon, freshly ground
- 2 cups vinegar
- 2 1/4 cups brown sugar
- 2 1/4 cups white sugar
- 1 Tablespoon ground cloves

Directions:

1. Cook the apples in a pan with cider and vinegar until tender.
2. Press through a strainer.
3. Cook the pulp with sugar and spices for a few minutes.
4. Fill into sterile half-pint or pint jars, leaving 1/4-inch of space.
5. Close the jars tightly, then heat for 5 minutes in a water bath.

24. Banana, Cherry & Pineapple Butter

MAKES: 4 half-pint jars

Ingredients:

- 1 cup canned crushed pineapple
- 2 tablespoon maraschino cherries, chopped
- 1 cup mashed banana
- 2 teaspoon lemon juice
- 3 ½ cups granulated sugar
- 3 oz. liquid pectin

Directions:

1. Combine all ingredients, except the pectin, in a saucepan and bring to boil, stirring continuously.
2. Turn-off heat and stir in the pectin for 5 minutes.
3. Skim-off any visible foam.
4. Fill into the sterilized jars, leaving quarter-inch of of space.
5. Remove air bubbles and clean the rims.
6. Put the lids on, followed by the bands.
7. Process jars in a water canner for 5 minutes.

25. Cinnamon Flavored Peach Butter

MAKES: 3 pint jars

Ingredients:

- 4 lbs. peaches, pitted, and quartered
- ¼ cup lemon juice
- 2 cups sugar
- 2 cups water
- 2 tablespoon grated lemon zest
- 2 teaspoon cinnamon

Directions:

1. Combine the water and peaches in a pan and bring to boil.
2. Simmer until tender, stirring frequently.
3. Process the mixture in batches till smooth.
4. Transfer the mixture into the pan again and mix in the lemon juice, lemon zest, sugar, and cinnamon.
5. Bring to boil again, stirring regularly.
6. Simmer for 30 minutes.
7. Turn the heat off; skim-off any foam.
8. Fill into the sterilized jars, leaving quarter-inch of of space.
9. Remove air bubbles and clean the rims.
10. Put the lids on, followed by the bands.
11. Process jars in a water canner for 10 minutes.

26. Cinnamon Banana Butter

MAKES: 2 11-ounce jars

Ingredients:

- ½ teaspoon ground cinnamon
- 3 oz. fruit pectin
- 3 teaspoons vanilla
- 4 ½ cups sugar
- 1/3 cup fresh lemon juice
- 4 cups mashed bananas

Directions:

1. In a saucepan, mix lemon juice, bananas, and pectin until the pectin is dissolved. Stir in the sugar and bring to a boil.
2. Stirring regularly heat to a full rolling boil; then remove the pan from heat and mix in vanilla and cinnamon.
3. Fill into sterilized jars, leaving 1/2-inch space.
4. Clean the rims and lids and secure on jars.
5. Put jars in a water bath for 10 minutes.

---

27. Hot Chili Pepper Butter

MAKES: 8 pint jars

Ingredients:

- 1 quart cider vinegar
- 1 quart home-made yellow mustard
- 6 cups sugar
- 40 hot chili peppers, seeded, and chopped
- 1 ¼ cups flour
- 1 teaspoon salt
- 1 ½ cups water

Directions:

1. Mix all ingredients in a pot and boil for 5 minutes, stirring continuously.
2. Turn the heat off; skim-off any foam.
3. Fill into the sterilized jars, leaving quarter-inch of of space.
4. Remove air bubbles and clean the rims.
5. Put the lids on, followed by the bands.
6. Process jars in a water canner for 10 minutes.

28. Mango Butter

MAKES: 6 pint jars

Ingredients:

- 6 ½ cups ripe mangoes, peeled, pitted, and chopped
- 3 tablespoon lemon juice
- 2 ½ cups sugar
- ¾ cup orange juice
- ½ cup water

Directions:

1. Combine the orange juice, mangoes and water in a pot and bring to boil.
2. Simmer for 35 minutes.
3. Sieve and return the mushy mango to the pan.
4. Add sugar and lemon juice.
5. Stir and then cook for another 30 minutes.
6. Remove any foam.
7. Fill into the sterilized jars, up to three-fourths full.
8. Remove air bubbles and clean the rims.
9. Put the lids on, followed by the bands.
10. Process jars in a water canner for 10 minutes.

---

29. Spiced Pear Butter

MAKES: 9 half-pint jars

Ingredients:

- 15 Bartlett pears, sliced
- 1 teaspoon cloves, ground
- 1 ½ teaspoon cinnamon, ground
- 2 cups water
- 2 tablespoon lemon juice
- 6 cups sugar
- ½ teaspoon ginger, ground

Directions:

1. Combine water and pears in a pan and cook covered until tender, about 30 minutes.
2. Press the tender pears in a colander.
3. Transfer the pear pulp back into the pan.
4. In a separate pan caramelize 1 ½ cups of water, stirring and then transfer it into the pear pulp.
5. Mix in the left over ingredients except the lemon juice and cook for around 45 minutes uncovered till thickened, stirring frequently.
6. Turn the heat off; skim-off any foam.
7. Fill into the sterilized jars, leaving quarter-inch of of space.
8. Remove air bubbles and clean the rims.
9. Put the lids on, followed by the bands.
10. Process jars in a water canner for 15 minutes.

CHAPTER 7: SALSAS AND RELISHES

30. Chayote Pear relish

Ingredients:

- 2 cups chopped red bell pepper
- 1 teaspoon ground pumpkin pie spice
- 2 teaspoons canning salt
- 3 cups chopped onion
- 3 1/2 cups peeled, cubed Seckel pears
- 3 1/2 cups chayote, peeled, seeded and cubed
- 2 Serrano peppers, chopped
- 1 teaspoon ground allspice
- 1 1/2 cups water
- 1 cup white sugar
- 2 1/2 cups cider 5% vinegar
- 2 cups chopped yellow bell pepper

Directions:

1. Boil vinegar, water, sugar, salt and spices in a Dutch oven.
2. Add chopped onions and peppers; return to a boil for 2 minutes, moving sporadically.
3. Add chayote and pears.
4. Ladle the solids into jars, leaving 1-inch of space.
5. Top with cooking liquid, leaving 1/2-inch of space.
6. Release air bubbles.
7. Close the jars tightly, then heat for 5 minutes in a water bath.

31. Mango Ginger salsa

Ingredients:

- 6 cups diced unripe mango
- 2 teaspoons chopped ginger
- 1 1/2 cups diced red bell pepper
- 1/2 cup yellow onion, chopped
- 1/2 cup water
- 1/4 cups cider 5% vinegar
- 1/2 teaspoons crushed red pepper flakes
- 2 teaspoons chopped garlic
- 1 cup brown sugar

Directions:

1. Mix ingredients in a Dutch oven or stockpot.
2. Boil on high, while stirring.
3. Simmer 5 minutes.
4. Fill into jars, leaving 1/2-inch of space.
5. Release air bubbles.
6. Close the jars tightly, then heat for 5 minutes in a water bath.

---

32. Pickle relish

Ingredients:

- 3 quarts chopped cucumbers
- 1 cup chopped onions
- 4 cups ice
- 8 cups water
- 3/4 cup pickling salt
- 6 cups of sweet green and red peppers, chopped
- 2 cups sugar
- 4 teaspoons of mustard seed
- 4 teaspoons of turmeric
- 4 teaspoons of turmeric
- 4 teaspoons of allspice
- 4 teaspoons of whole cloves
- 6 cups 5% white vinegar

Directions:

1. Add cucumbers, peppers, onions, salt, and ice to water and set aside for 4 hours. Drain.
2. Combine spices in a spice or cheesecloth bag. Add spices to sugar and vinegar. Bring to a steaming boil and pour mixture over vegetables.
3. Cover and refrigerate 24 hours.

4. Boil mixture and then transfer to jars, leaving 1/2-inch of space.
5. Release air bubbles.
6. Close the jars tightly, then heat for 5 minutes in a water bath.

---

33. Pickled corn and peppers relish

Ingredients:

- 2 1/2 cups diced sweet red peppers
- 2 1/2 Tablespoons dry mustard
- 1-3/4 cups sugar
- 2 1/2 cups diced sweet green peppers
- 2 1/2 cups chopped celery
- 1/4 cups diced onions
- 10 cups fresh whole kernel corn, boiled
- 5 cups 5% vinegar
- 2 1/2 Tablespoons pickling salt
- 2 1/2 teaspoons celery seed
- 1/4 teaspoons turmeric

Directions:

1. Combine all peppers, celery, onions, sugar, vinegar, salt, and celery seed in a pan.
2. Bring to boil and simmer 5 minutes, moving sporadically.
3. Combine turmeric, mustard and 1/2 cup of the mixture.
4. Combine everything and simmer for 5 minutes.
5. Thicken mixture with lour paste and stir frequently. Fill hot jars with hot mixture, leaving 1/2-inch of space.
6. Release air bubbles.
7. Close the jars tightly, then heat for 5 minutes in a water bath.

---

34. Pickled green tomato relish

Ingredients:

- 1 1/2 lbs. red bell peppers, washed and chopped
- 2 lbs. onions, washed and chopped
- 1/2 cup pickling salt
- 10 lbs. green tomatoes, washed and chopped
- 1-quart water
- 4 cups sugar
- 1 1/2 lbs. green bell peppers, washed and chopped
- 1-quart 5% vinegar
- 1/3 cup home-made yellow mustard
- 2 Tablespoons cornstarch

Directions:

1. Dissolve salt and pour over vegetables.
2. Bring to a boil and simmer 5 minutes.
3. Drain in colander. Return vegetables to kettle.
4. Add sugar, vinegar, mustard, and cornstarch. Stir to mix. Bring to a steaming boil and simmer 5 minutes.
5. Fill hot sterile pint jars with hot relish, leaving 1/2-inch of space.
6. Release air bubbles.
7. Close the jars tightly, then heat for 5 minutes in a water bath.

---

35. Pickled pepper-onion relish

Ingredients:

- 6 cups chopped onions
- 3 cups chopped green peppers
- 1 1/2 cups sugar
- 3 cups chopped sweet red peppers
- 6 cups 5% vinegar, preferably white distilled
- 2 Tablespoons pickling salt

Directions:

1. Combine all Ingredients and boil until mixture thickens, about 30 minutes.
2. Ladle jars with hot relish, leaving 1/2-inch of space, and seal tightly.

---

36. Spiced Peach apple salsa

Ingredients:

- 6 cups chopped Roma tomatoes, washed and peeled
- 2 1/2 cups diced yellow onions
- 10 cups chopped hard, unripe peaches
- 2 cups chopped Granny Smith apples, cored
- 4 Tablespoons mixed pickling spice
- 2 1/4 cups cider 5% vinegar
- 1 Tablespoon canning salt
- 2 teaspoons crushed red pepper flakes
- 3 3/4 cups brown sugar
- 2 cups chopped green bell peppers

Directions:

1. Place pickling spice on a double-layered cheese-cloth. Bring corners together and tie.
2. Combine chopped tomatoes, onions and peppers in a Dutch oven or sauce-pot.
3. Immerse peaches for 10 minutes in an ascorbic acid solution.
4. Immerse apples for 10 minutes in ascorbic acid solution.
5. Add chopped peaches and apples to the sauce-pot with the vegetables.
6. Add the spice bag, salt, pepper flakes, brown sugar and vinegar.
7. Simmer 30 minutes, moving sporadically.
8. Remove spice bag and discard.
9. Fill salsa solids into hot pint jars, leaving 1/4-inch of space.
10. Cover with cooking liquid, leaving 1/2-inch of space.
11. Release air bubbles.
12. Close the jars tightly, then heat for 5 minutes in a water bath.

---

37. Spicy Cinnamon jicama relish

Ingredients:

- 9 cups diced jicama
- 1 two-inch stick cinnamon
- 4 cups chopped onion
- 4 cups sugar
- 2 teaspoons crushed red pepper
- 4 cups diced yellow bell pepper
- 8 cups 5% white vinegar
- 1 Tablespoon whole mixed pickling spice
- 4 1/2 cups diced red bell pepper
- 2 fresh finger-hot peppers, chopped and partially seeded

Directions:

1. Place pickling spice and cinnamon on a double-layered cheesecloth.
2. Fold and tie with a string.
3. In a Dutch oven or sauce-pot, combine pickling spice bag, vinegar, sugar, and crushed red pepper. Boil, stirring to dissolve sugar.
4. Stir in jicama, peppers, onion and finger-hots. Return mixture to boiling.
5. Simmer, covered, over low heat about 25 minutes. Discard spice bag.
6. Fill into hot pint jars, leaving 1/2-inch of space. Cover with hot pickling liquid, leaving 1/2-inch of space.
7. Release air bubbles.
8. Close the jars tightly, then heat for 5 minutes in a water bath.

38. Spicy cranberry pepper salsa

Ingredients:

- 6 cups chopped red onion
- 1 1/2 cups water
- 1 1/2 cups cider 5% vinegar
- 1 Tablespoon canning salt
- 4 chopped large Serrano peppers
- 1/3 cups sugar
- 6 Tablespoons clover honey
- 12 cups rinsed, fresh whole cranberries

Directions:

1. Combine all Ingredients except cranberries using a Dutch oven. Boil on high; Simmer for 5 minutes.
2. Add cranberries, simmer mixture for 20 minutes, moving sporadically to prevent scorching.
3. Fill the hot mixture into hot pint jars, leaving 1/4-inch of space.
4. Release air bubbles.
5. Close the jars tightly, then heat for 5 minutes in a water bath.

---

39. Tangy tomatillo relish

Ingredients:

- 12 cups chopped tomatillos, husks removed and washed
- 3 cups chopped jicama
- 6 1/2 cups cider 5% vinegar
- 3 cups chopped onion
- 1 Tablespoon crushed red pepper flakes
- 2 quarts water
- 6 cups sugar
- 1 1/2 cups chopped red bell pepper
- 1 1/2 cups chopped yellow bell pepper
- 1 cup canning salt
- 6 Tablespoons whole mixed pickling spice
- 6 cups chopped plum-type tomatoes
- 1 1/2 cups chopped green bell pepper

Directions:

1. Place all vegetables in a Dutch oven.
2. Dissolve canning salt in water. Pour over vegetables.
3. Bring to a steaming boil; simmer 5 minutes.
4. Drain through a cheesecloth-lined strainer.
5. Fill the hot mixture into hot pint jars, leaving 1/4-inch of space.
6. Release air bubbles.
7. Close the jars tightly, then heat for 5 minutes in a water bath.

CHAPTER 8: MEAT

40. Apricot Pork

MAKES: 4

Ingredients:

- 1/2 teaspoon salt
- 1/2 teaspoon dried thyme
- 1 pound canned pork
- 2 tablespoons olive oil
- 1 sliced onion
- 1 tablespoons butter
- 2 tablespoons apricot jam
- 1/2 cup chicken broth
- 1 tablespoons Dijon mustard

Directions:

1. Sprinkle pork with salt and thyme on both sides.

2. Brown pork for 3 minutes per side.
3. Remove from skillet, and then melt butter in skillet.
4. Cook onion for 3 minutes. After which, add jam, mustard, and broth.
5. Bring to a boil, stirring continuously.
6. Cover and turn heat to low, then simmer for 5 minutes.
7. Return pork to skillet and stir to coat in sauce.
8. Again, cover and simmer for at least 5 minutes more to heat pork through.

---

41. Beef Stew

MAKES: 4

Ingredients:

- 3 tablespoons flour
- 2 pounds canned beef
- 1 package beef stew seasoning mix powder
- 2 tablespoons vegetable oil
- 5 cups frozen bagged vegetables
- 3 cups water

Directions:

1. Toss beef in flour, then browns in oil in a skillet.
2. Stir in water and seasoning.
3. Add frozen vegetables; bring to a steaming boil.
4. Simmer for 15 minutes, covered.

42. Canned Beef Stroganoff

MAKES: 6

Ingredients:

- 1-teaspoon black pepper
- 2 teaspoons salt
- 2 teaspoons thyme
- 2 teaspoons parsley
- 4 tablespoons Worcestershire sauce
- 2 cloves of garlic, minced
- 1 cup mushrooms, sliced
- 1 cup onion, chopped
- 2 pounds stewing beef, cut into chunks
- 4 cups beef broth
-

Directions:

1. Place all the needed ingredients in a pot; bring to a steaming boil for 5 minutes. Reduce the heat and allow simmering for another 20 minutes
2. Transfer mixture to sterilized bottles.
3. Release air bubbles and close jars.
4. Place the jars in pressure canner and process for 25 minutes.

---

43. Canned Chili

MAKES: 6

Ingredients:

- 3 cups of dry kidney beans, soaked overnight and boiled
- 2 pounds ground beef
- 1 cup onion, chopped
- 1 cup pepper, seeded and chopped
- 4 cups tomatoes, chopped
- 1 tablespoon chili pepper, seeded and chopped

Directions:

1. Put the cooked beans and the other ingredients to a pot. Cook for another 20 minutes.
2. Transfer the mixture into the sterilized bottles. Leave an inch of of space.
3. Release air bubbles and close jars.
4. Place the jars in pressure canner and process for 25 minutes. Follow the guidelines for pressure canning.

44. Pork jelly

Ingredients:

- 1/2 pork head
- 3 kg mixed pork
- 5 bay leaves
- 5 garlic cloves
- 1/2 litre vinegar
- Pinch ground red pepper
- Pinch salt

Directions:

1. Cut the head into large pieces and wash it, cut the meat and wash it, cover everything with cold water and boil.
2. When the meat is cold cut into small pieces eliminating the bones.

3. Put the meat in a pot, with cooking water and remaining ingredients.
4. Cook for 1/2 hour; put in the containers.

45. Grilled Venison

MAKES: 4

Ingredients:

- 2 pounds canned venison
- 1 -1/2 pounds sliced bacon
- 1-quart apple cider
- 24 oz. bottled barbecue sauce or marinade

Directions:

1. Place venison on a shallow baking dish and cover in apple cider.
2. Refrigerate for at least2 hours.
3. Remove and pat the meat dry, then discard apple cider and place venison back in baking dish.
4. Pour barbecue sauce over venison, cover and let marinate.
5. Preheat an outdoor grill.
6. Remove the meat from the refrigerator then let it stand for 30 minutes.
7. Wrap pieces of venison in bacon.
8. Place bacon-wrapped venison pieces onto grill grate, not touching each other.
9. Grill for 20 minutes, regularly turning it.

46. Ground/Chopped Beef, Pork, Lamb, or Sausage

MAKES: 2

Ingredients:

- Preferred meat, fresh, chilled, chopped/ground
- Salt
- Meat broth, boiling/tomato juice/water

Directions:

1. Chop the chilled fresh meat into small chunks. If using venison, grind after mixing with one cup of pork fat to every three to four cups of venison. If using sausage, combine with cayenne pepper and salt.
2. Shape into meatballs or patties. If using cased sausage, chop into three to four -inch links.
3. Cook the meat until brown in color. If using ground meat, sauté without shaping.

4. Add the cooked meat to clean and hot Mason jars. Each filled with salt.
5. Boil the meat broth. Pour the meat broth, tomato juice, or water into the jars until filled up to one inch from the top.
6. Release air bubbles before adjusting the lids, then process in the pressure canner for 1 hour and 15 minutes.

---

47. Italian Beef

MAKES: 4

Ingredients:

- 4 toasted baguettes
- 16oz beef broth
- 1 pound canned beef
- Toppings like peppers, onions, and cheese

Directions:

1. Brown beef for 5 minutes per side in the skillet.
2. Add broth; bring to a steaming boil.
3. After this, turn heat to low and simmer until slightly reduced.
4. Spoon onto baguettes.
5. Top with toppings of your choice.

CHAPTER 9: FRUITS AND VEGETABLES

48. Bread-and-butter pickles

Ingredients:

- 8 cups thinly sliced onions
- 2 Tablespoons mustard seed
- 1/2 cup pickling salt
- 4 cups 5% vinegar
- 1 1/2 Tablespoons celery seed
- 1 cup pickling lime
- 6 lbs. of cucumbers, washed and sliced
- 4 1/2 cups sugar
- 1 Tablespoon ground turmeric

Directions:

1. Toss cucumbers and onions with salt in a large bowl.
2. Cover with ice and refrigerate 4 hours,.
3. Combine remaining Ingredients in a pot.

4. Boil 10 minutes.
5. Drain and add cucumbers and onions and bring to a steaming boil.
6. Fill jars with mixture, leaving 1/2-inch of space. Release air bubbles.
7. Close the jars tightly, then heat for 5 minutes in a water bath.

---

49. Chayote and jicama slaw

Ingredients:

- 4 cups julienned jicama
- 1 teaspoon celery seed
- 2 cups chopped red bell pepper
- 1/2 cup white sugar
- 2 chopped hot peppers
- 4 cups julienned chayote
- 23 1/2 teaspoons canning salt
- 1/2 cups water
- 2 1/2 cups cider 5% vinegar

Directions:

1. In a stockpot, combine all Ingredients except chayote. Bring to a boil for 5 minutes.
2. Add chayote.
3. Bring back to a boil and then turn heat of. Fill into jars, leaving 1/2-inch of space.
4. Top with cooking liquid, leaving 1/2-inch of space.
5. Release air bubbles.
6. Close the jars tightly, then heat for 5 minutes in a water bath.

50. Cantaloupe pickles

MAKES: ABOUT 4 PINT JARS

Ingredients:

- 5 lbs. of 1-inch cantaloupe cubes
- 1 teaspoon crushed red pepper flakes
- 2 cinnamon sticks
- 2 teaspoons ground cloves
- 1 teaspoon ground ginger
- 4 1/2 cups cider 5% vinegar
- 2cups water
- 1 1/2 cups white sugar
- 1 1/2 cups brown sugar

Directions:

DAY ONE:
1. Place cantaloupe, pepper flakes, cinnamon sticks, cloves and ginger in a spice bag and tie the ends.
2. Combine vinegar and water in a stockpot. Bring to a boil.
3. Add spice bag and steep for 5 minutes, moving sporadically.
4. Pour over melon pieces in the bowl.
5. Refrigerate overnight.

DAY TWO:
6. Pour vinegar solution into a saucepan; bring to a steaming boil.
7. Add sugar, cantaloupe and bring back to a boil.
8. Simmer, about 1 to 1/4 hours. Set aside.
9. Bring remaining liquid to a boil an additional 5 minutes.
10. Add the cantaloupe, and bring back to a boil.
11. Ladle pieces into hot pint jars, leaving 1-inch of space.
12. Top with boiling hot syrup, leaving 1/2-inch of space.
13. Release air bubbles.
14. Close the jars tightly, then heat for 5 minutes in a water bath.

---

51. Dill pickles

Ingredients:
- 4 lbs. of 4-inch pickling cucumber, washed and sliced
- 2 Tablespoons dill seed
- 1/2 cup salt
- 1/4 cup 5% vinegar
- 8 cups water
- 2 cloves garlic
- 2 teaspoons whole mixed pickling spices

Directions:
1. Place half of dill and spices on a container.
2. Add cucumbers, remaining dill, and spices.
3. Dissolve salt in vinegar and water and pour over cucumbers.
4. Add suitable cover and weight.
5. Store to ferment where temperature is between 70° and 75°F for about 4 weeks.
6. Fill hot jar with pickles and hot brine, leaving 1/2-inch of space.
7. Release air bubbles.
8. Close the jars tightly, then heat for 5 minutes in a water bath.

52. Marinated whole mushrooms

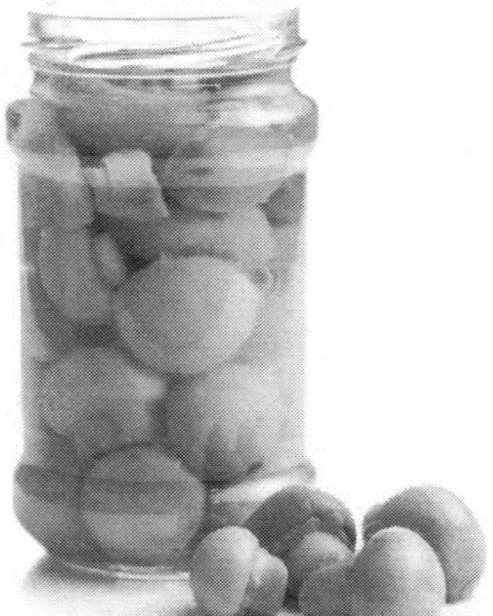

Ingredients:

- 7 lbs. small whole mushrooms, washed
- 25 black peppercorns
- 2 cloves garlic, cut in quarters
- 1/4 cup diced pimiento
- 1 Tablespoon dried basil leaves
- 2 cups olive or salad oil
- 1 Tablespoon oregano leaves
- 1/2 cup chopped onions
- 1/2 cup bottled lemon juice
- 1 Tablespoon pickling salt
- 2 1/2 cups 5% white vinegar

Directions:

1. Add lemon juice and water to cover mushrooms. Bring to boil and then drain mushrooms.
2. Mix olive oil, vinegar, oregano, basil, salt, onions and pimiento and bring to a steaming boil.
3. Place 1/4 garlic clove and 2 peppercorns in a half-pint jar.
4. Fill with mushrooms and oil/vinegar solution, leaving 1/2-inch of space.
5. Release air bubbles.
6. Close the jars tightly, then heat for 5 minutes in a water bath.

---

53. Marinated Oregano peppers

Ingredients:

- 4 lbs. firm peppers (Bell, Hungarian, banana, or jalapeño pepper)
- 1 cup bottled lemon juice
- 2 cups 5% white vinegar
- 1 Tablespoon oregano leaves
- 1/2 cup chopped onions
- 2 Tablespoons horseradish
- 1 cup olive oil
- 2 cloves garlic, quartered

Directions:

1. Blister peppers on a burner until skins blister.
2. Place blistered peppers in a pan and cover with a damp cloth.
3. Cool and peel of skins.
4. Mix all remaining Ingredients in a saucepan and Bring to a steaming boil.
5. Place 1/4 garlic clove and 1/4 teaspoon salt in each jar.
6. Fill hot jars with peppers.
7. Top with hot oil/pickling solution, leaving 1/2-inch of space.
8. Release air bubbles.
9. Close the jars tightly, then heat for 5 minutes in a water bath.

---

54. Mixed fruit cocktail

Ingredients:

- 3 lbs. peaches
- 3 lbs. Pears, Peeled, halved, cored, and cubed
- 1 1/2 lbs. under-ripe seedless green grape
- 10-oz jar of maraschino cherries
- 3 cups sugar
- 4 cups water

Directions:

1. Immerse grapes in ascorbic acid solution.
2. Dip peaches in boiling water for 1 minute to loosen skins.
3. Peel off skins. Cut in half, cube and keep in solution with grapes.
4. Add pears.
5. Drain mixed fruit. .
6. Boil sugar and water in a pan. Add 1/2 cup of hot syrup to each hot jar
7. Then add a few cherries and gently fill the jar with mixed fruit and more hot syrup, leaving 1/2-inch of space.
8. Release air bubbles.
9. Close the jars tightly, then heat for 5 minutes in a water bath.

---

55. No sugar added pickled beets

Ingredients:

- 7 lbs. of beets, trimmed, boiled, peeled and sliced
- 6 onions, sliced
- 6 cups white vinegar
- 1 1/2 teaspoons pickling salt
- 2 cups Splenda
- 3 cups water
- 2 cinnamon sticks
- 12 whole cloves

Directions:

1. Combine vinegar, salt, Splenda, and 3 cups fresh water in Dutch oven.
2. Tie cinnamon sticks and cloves in cheesecloth bag and add to vinegar mixture.
3. Bring to a boil and then add beets and onions; simmer 5 minutes.
4. Remove spice bag.
5. Ladle beets and onion into hot pint jars, leaving 1/2-inch of space.
6. Top with boiling vinegar solution, leaving 1/2-inch of space.
7. Release air bubbles.
8. Close the jars tightly, then heat for 5 minutes in a water bath.

56. Pickled spicy green tomatoes

Ingredients:

- 10 to 11 lbs. of green tomatoes, sliced
- 2 cups sliced onions
- 1/4 cup pickling salt
- 3 cups brown sugar
- 4 cups 5% vinegar
- 1 Tablespoon mustard seed
- 1 Tablespoon allspice
- 1 Tablespoon celery seed
- 1 Tablespoon whole cloves

Directions:

1. Place tomatoes and onions in bowl; sprinkle with
2. 1/4 salt, and leave 6 hours. Drain.
3. Add sugar/vinegar mixture until dissolved.
4. Tie all spices in a spice bag. Add to vinegar with tomatoes and onions.
5. Bring to boil and simmer 30 minutes, stirring.
6. Remove spice bag.
7. Fill jar with solids and cover with hot pickling solution, leaving 1/2-inch of space.
8. Release air bubbles.
9. Close the jars tightly, then heat for 5 minutes in a water bath.

57. Pickled mixed vegetables

Ingredients:

- 4 lbs. of pickling cucumbers
- 4 cups cut celery
- 2 cups peeled and cut carrots
- 2 cups cut sweet red peppers
- 2 cups cauliflower flowerets
- 3 Tablespoons celery seed
- 2 lbs. peeled onions, quartered
- 5 cups 5% white vinegar
- 1/4 cup home-made mustard
- 1/2 cup pickling salt
- 3 1/2 cups sugar
- 2 Tablespoons mustard seed
- 1/2 teaspoons whole cloves
- 1/2 teaspoons ground turmeric

Directions:

1. Combine vegetables, cover with 2 inches of cubed or crushed ice, and refrigerate 3 to 4 hours.
2. Combine vinegar and mustard and mix well.
3. Add salt, sugar, celery seed, mustard seed, cloves, turmeric and bring to a boil.
4. Drain and add to hot pickling solution.
5. Cover and slowly bring to boil. Drain vegetables but save pickling solution. Fill vegetables in hot sterile pint jars, or hot quarts, leaving 1/2-inch of space. Add pickling solution, leaving 1/2-inch of space.
6. Release air bubbles.
7. Close the jars tightly, then heat for 5 minutes in a water bath.

58. Pickled bread-and-butter zucchini

Ingredients:

- 16 cups fresh zucchini, sliced
- 4 cups onions, thinly sliced
- 1/2 cup pickling salt
- 4 cups 5% white vinegar
- 2 cups sugar
- 4 Tablespoons mustard seed
- 2 Tablespoons celery seed
- 2 teaspoons ground turmeric

Directions:

1. Cover zucchini and onion slices with water and salt. Leave for 2 hours.

2. Mix vinegar, sugar, and spices. Bring to a boil and add zucchini and onions. Simmer another 5 minutes.
3. Ladle mixture and pickling solution in hot jars, leaving 1/2-inch of space.
4. Release air bubbles.
5. Close the jars tightly, then heat for 5 minutes in a water bath.

59. Pickled asparagus

Ingredients:

- 10 lbs. Asparagus spears
- 6 large garlic cloves, peeled
- 4 1/2 cups water
- 4 1/2 cups 5% white distilled vinegar
- 6 small hot peppers
- 1/2 cup canning salt
- 3 teaspoons dill seed

Directions:

1. Place a garlic clove at the bottom of each jar, and tightly pack asparagus into hot jars with the blunt ends down. In a sauce-pot, combine water, vinegar, hot peppers, salt and dill seed.
2. Bring to a boil. Place one hot pepper in each jar over asparagus spears. Pour boiling hot pickling brine over spears, leaving 1/2-inch of space.
3. Release air bubbles.
4. Close the jars tightly, then heat for 5 minutes in a water bath.

60. Pickled dilled beans

Ingredients:

- 4 lbs. fresh tender green or yellow beans
- 8 to 16 heads fresh dill
- 8 cloves garlic
- 1/2 cup pickling salt
- 4 cups 5% white vinegar
- 4 cups water
- 1 teaspoon hot red pepper lakes

Directions:

1. Wash and trim ends from beans and cut to 4-inch lengths. In each hot sterile pint jar, place 1 to 2 dill heads and, 1 clove of garlic. Place whole beans upright in jars, leaving 1/2-inch of space.
2. Trim beans to ensure proper it, if necessary. Combine salt, vinegar, water, and pepper flakes.
3. Bring to a boil. Add hot solution to beans, leaving 1/2-inch of space.
4. Release air bubbles.

5. Close the jars tightly, then heat for 5 minutes in a water bath.

61. Pickled beets

Ingredients:

- 7 lbs. of beets
- 4 cups 5% vinegar
- 1-2 teaspoons pickling salt
- 2 cups sugar
- 2 cups water
- 2 cinnamon sticks
- 12 whole cloves
- 4 onions, Peeled and thinly sliced

Directions:

1. Cook beets until tender, about 25 minutes.
2. Cool beets and slip of skins. Slice beets.
3. Combine vinegar, salt, sugar, and fresh water.
4. Tie spices in cheesecloth bag and add to the mixture.
5. Add beets and onions. Simmer 5 minutes.
6. Remove spice bag.
7. Fill hot jars with beets and onions, leaving 1/2-inch of space. Add hot vinegar solution, allowing 1/2-inch of space.
8. Release air bubbles.
9. Close the jars tightly, then heat for 5 minutes in a water bath.

62. Pickled carrots

Ingredients:

- 2-3/4 lbs. peeled and sliced carrots
- 5 1/2 cups 5% white vinegar
- 1 cup water
- 2 cups sugar
- 2 teaspoons canning salt
- 8 teaspoons mustard seed
- 4 teaspoons celery seed

Directions:

1. Boil and stir vinegar, water, sugar and canning salt in a Dutch oven for 3 minutes. Add carrots and bring back to a boil. Simmer, about 10 minutes.
2. Meanwhile, place 2 teaspoons mustard seed and 1 teaspoon celery seed into each empty hot pint jar. Fill jars with hot carrots, leaving 1-inch of space. Fill with hot pickling liquid, leaving 1/2-inch of space.

3. Release air bubbles.
4. Close the jars tightly, then heat for 5 minutes in a water bath.

---

63. Pickled cauliflower/Brussels

Ingredients:

- 2 Tablespoons mustard seed
- 1 teaspoon hot red pepper lakes
- 12 cups of cauliflower or Brussels, boiled in salt water
- 4 cups 5% white vinegar
- 1 cup diced sweet red peppers
- 2 cups sugar
- 2 cups thinly sliced onions
- 1 Tablespoon celery seed
- 1 teaspoon turmeric

Directions:

1. Combine vinegar, sugar, onion, diced red pepper, and spices in pan.
2. Simmer 5 minutes. Distribute onion and diced pepper among jars. Fill hot jars with pieces and pickling solution, leaving 1/2-inch of space.
3. Release air bubbles.
4. Close the jars tightly, then heat for 5 minutes in a water bath.

---

64. Pickled dilled okra

Ingredients:

- 6 small hot peppers
- 4 teaspoons dill seed
- 8 to 9 garlic cloves
- 7 lbs. okra pods
- 2/3 cup pickling salt
- 6 cups water
- 6 cups 5% vinegar

Directions:

1. Wash and trim okra. Fill hot jars with whole okra, leaving 1/2-inch of space. Place 1 garlic clove in each jar.
2. Combine salt, hot peppers, dill seed, water, and vinegar in pan; bring to a steaming boil.
3. Ladle pickling solution over okra, leaving 1/2-inch of space.
4. Release air bubbles.

5. Close the jars tightly, then heat for 5 minutes in a water bath.

---

65. Pickled pearl onions with mustard

Ingredients:

- 8 cups peeled white pearl onions
- 5 1/2 cups 5% white vinegar
- 1 cup water
- 2 teaspoons canning salt
- 2 cups sugar
- 8 teaspoons mustard seed
- 4 teaspoons celery seed

Directions:

1. Combine vinegar, water, salt and sugar in a Dutch oven or stockpot. Bring to a boil 3 minutes.
2. Add peeled onions and bring back to a boil. Simmer, about 5 minutes.
3. Meanwhile, place 2 teaspoons mustard seed and 1 teaspoon celery seed into each empty hot pint jar. Fill with hot onions, leaving 1-inch of space. Fill with hot pickling liquid, leaving 1/2-inch of space.
4. Release air bubbles.
5. Close the jars tightly, then heat for 5 minutes in a water bath.

---

66. Pickled bell peppers

Ingredients:

- 7 lbs. firm bell peppers, seeded and diced into strips
- 3 1/2 cups sugar
- 3 cups 5% vinegar
- 3 cups water
- 9 cloves garlic
- 4 1/2 teaspoons pickling salt

Directions:

1. Boil sugar, vinegar, and water for 1 minute.
2. Add peppers; bring to a steaming boil.
3. Place 1/2 clove of garlic and 1/4 teaspoon salt in each jar.
4. Add pepper strips and cover with hot vinegar mixture, leaving 1/2-inch space.

67. Pickled hot peppers

Ingredients:

- 4 lbs. hot peppers (Hungarian, banana, chile or jalapeño)
- 5 cups 5% vinegar
- 1 cup water
- 4 teaspoons pickling salt
- 3 lbs. sweet red and green peppers, quartered
- 2 Tablespoons sugar
- 2 cloves garlic

Directions:

1. Blister peppers on a burner.
2. Place peppers in a pan and cover with a damp cloth.
3. Cool several minutes; peel of skins. Flatten small peppers. Quarter large peppers. Fill hot jars with peppers, leaving 1/2-inch of space.
4. Heat other Ingredients to boiling and simmer 10 minutes.
5. Discard garlic.
6. Add hot pickling solution over peppers, leaving 1/2-inch of space.
7. Release air bubbles.
8. Close the jars tightly, then heat for 5 minutes in a water bath.

68. Pickled jalapeño pepper rings

Ingredients:

- 3 lbs. jalapeño peppers, sliced
- 1 1/2 gallons water
- 71/2 cups cider 5% vinegar
- 2 cups water
- 2 1/2 Tablespoons canning salt
- 1 1/2 cups pickling lime
- 3 Tablespoons celery seed
- 6 Tablespoons mustard seed

Directions:

1. Mix pickling lime with 1 1/2 gallons water.
2. Immerse pepper slices in the lime water, in refrigerator, for 18 hours, moving sporadically.
3. Drain lime solution from soaked pepper rings.
4. Place 1 tablespoon mustard seed and 1 1/2 teaspoons celery seed in the bottom of each hot pint jar.
5. Pack drained pepper rings into the jars, leaving 1/2-inch of space. Bring cider vinegar, water and canning salt to a boil on high.
6. Ladle brine over pepper rings in jars, leaving 1/2-inch of space.
7. Release air bubbles.

8. Close the jars tightly, then heat for 5 minutes in a water bath.

69. Pickled yellow pepper rings

Ingredients:

- 2 1/2 to 3 lbs. yellow peppers, sliced into rings
- 2 Tablespoons celery seed
- 4 Tablespoons mustard seed
- 5 cups cider 5% vinegar
- 1/4 cups water
- 5 teaspoons canning salt

Directions:

1. Place 1/2 tablespoon celery seed and 1 tablespoon mustard seed in each jar.
2. Fill pepper rings into jars, leaving 1/2-inch of space.
3. In a Dutch oven, combine the cider vinegar, water and salt; Bring to a steaming boil.
4. Ladle pepper rings into jars and top with boiling pickling liquid, leaving 1/2-inch of space.
5. Release air bubbles.
6. Close the jars tightly, then heat for 5 minutes in a water bath.

70. Piccalilli

Ingredients:

- 6 cups chopped green tomatoes
- 1 1/2 cups green peppers, chopped
- 7 1/2 cups chopped cabbage
- 1/2 cup pickling salt
- 1 1/2 cups sweet red peppers, chopped
- 2 1/4 cups chopped onions
- 3 Tablespoons whole mixed pickling spice
- 4 1/2 cups 5% vinegar
- 3 cups brown sugar

Directions:

1. Toss vegetables with 1/2 cup salt.
2. Cover with hot water and leave for12 hours. Drain.
3. Tie spices in a spice bag and add to combined vinegar and brown sugar and heat to a boil in a sauce pan.
4. Add vegetables and boil gently 30 minutes; remove spice bag.

5. Fill hot sterile jars, with hot mixture, leaving 1/2-inch of space.
6. Release air bubbles.
7. Close the jars tightly, then heat for 5 minutes in a water bath.

71. Quick sweet pickles

Ingredients:

- 8 lbs. of 3- to 4-inch pickling cucumbers
- 1/3 cup pickling salt
- 4 1/2 cups sugar
- 3 1/2 cups 5% vinegar
- 2 teaspoons celery seed
- 1 Tablespoon whole allspice
- 2 Tablespoons mustard seed
- 1 cup pickling lime

Directions:

1. Wash cucumbers. Cut 1/16-inch of blossom end and discard, but leave 1/4 inch of stem attached. Slice or cut in strips. Place in bowl and sprinkle with 1/3 cup salt. Cover with ice.
2. Refrigerate 3 to 4 hours. Add more ice as needed. Drain well.
3. Combine sugar, vinegar, celery seed, allspice, and mustard seed in a kettle. Bring to a steaming boil.
4. Hot pack—Add cucumbers and heat slowly until vinegar solution returns to boil.
5. Fill sterile jars, leaving 1/2-inch of space.
6. Raw pack—Fill hot jars, leaving 1/2-inch of space. Add hot pickling syrup, leaving 1/2-inch of space.
7. Release air bubbles.
8. Close the jars tightly, then heat for 5 minutes in a water bath.

72. Sweet pickle cucumber

Ingredients:

- 3 1/2 lbs. of pickling cucumbers, cleaned and sliced
- boiling water to cover sliced cucumbers
- 4 cups cider 5% vinegar
- 1 cup water
- 3 cups Splenda
- 1 Tablespoon canning salt
- 1 Tablespoon mustard seed
- 1 Tablespoon whole allspice
- 1 Tablespoon celery seed
- 4 cinnamon sticks

Directions:

1. Pour boiling water over the cucumber slices and leave for5 to 10 minutes.

2. Drain of the hot water and pour cold water over the cucumbers.
3. Mix vinegar, 1 cup water, Splenda and all spices in a Dutch oven or stockpot. Bring to a boil.
4. Add drained cucumber slices.
5. Drop a cinnamon stick in each jar.
6. Fill hot pickle slices into hot pint jars, leaving 1/2-inch of space.
7. Top with boiling pickling brine, leaving 1/2-inch of space.
8. Release air bubbles.
9. Close the jars tightly, then heat for 5 minutes in a water bath.

---

73. Sliced dill pickles

Ingredients:

- 4 lbs. pickling cucumbers
- 1 1/2 teaspoons celery seed
- 6 cups 5% vinegar
- 6 cups sugar
- 2 Tablespoons pickling salt
- 8 heads fresh dill
- 1 1/2 teaspoons mustard seed
- 2 large onions, thinly sliced

Directions:

1. Wash cucumbers. Cut 1/16-inch slice of blossom end and discard. Cut cucumbers in 1/4-inch slices. Combine vinegar, sugar, salt, celery, and mustard seeds in pan. Bring mixture to boiling.
2. Place 2 slices of onion and 1/2 dill head on bottom of each hot pint jar. Fill hot jars with cucumber slices, leaving 1/2-inch of space.
3. Add 1 slice of onion and 1/2 dill head on top. Pour hot pickling solution over cucumbers, leaving 1/4-inch of space.
4. Release air bubbles.
5. Close the jars tightly, then heat for 5 minutes in a water bath.

---

74. Sliced sweet pickles

Ingredients:

- 4 lbs. pickling cucumbers

Brining solution:

- 1 quart distilled 5% white vinegar
- 1 Tablespoon mustard seed
- 1 Tablespoon pickling salt
- 1/2 cup sugar

Canning syrup:

- 1 2/3 cups distilled 5% white vinegar
- 3 cups sugar
- 1 Tablespoon whole allspice
- 2 1/4 teaspoons celery seed

Directions:

1. Wash cucumbers and cut 1/16 inch of blossom end, and discard. Cut cucumbers into 1/4-inch slices. Combine all Ingredients for canning syrup in a saucepan and Boil. Keep syrup hot until used.
2. In a large kettle, mix the Ingredients for the brining solution. Add the cut cucumbers, cover, and simmer until the cucumbers change color from bright to dull green, about 6 minutes. Drain the cucumber slices.
3. Fill hot jars, and cover with hot canning syrup leaving 1/2-inch of space.
4. Release air bubbles.
5. Close the jars tightly, then heat for 5 minutes in a water bath.

75. Sauerkraut

Ingredients:

- 25 lbs. Cabbage, rinsed and shredded
- 3/4 cup pickling salt

Directions:

1. Put cabbage in a container and add 3 tablespoons of salt.
2. Mix using clean hands.
3. Pack until salt draws juices from cabbage.
4. Add plate and weights; cover container with a clean bath towel.
5. Store at 70° to 75°F for 3 to 4 weeks.

76. Spiced apple rings

Ingredients:

- 12 lbs. firm tart apples, washed, sliced and cored
- 12 cups sugar
- 6 cups water
- 1/4 cups 5% white vinegar
- 8 cinnamon sticks
- 3 Tablespoons whole cloves
- 1 teaspoon red food coloring

Directions:

1. Immerse apples in ascorbic acid solution.
2. Combine sugar, water, vinegar, cloves, cinnamon candies, or cinnamon sticks and food coloring in a saucepan.
3. Stir and simmer 3 minutes.
4. Drain apples, add to hot syrup, and cook 5 minutes. Fill hot jars with apple rings and hot flavored syrup, leaving 1/2-inch of space.
5. Release air bubbles.
6. Close the jars tightly, then heat for 5 minutes in a water bath.

---

77. Spiced crab apples

Ingredients:

- 5 lbs. crab apples, blossom petals removed but stems attached
- 4 1/2 cups apple cider 5% vinegar
- 3 3/4 cups water
- 7 1/2 cups sugar
- 4 teaspoons whole cloves
- 4 sticks cinnamon
- Six 1/2-inch cubes of fresh ginger root

Directions:

1. Mix vinegar, water, and sugar; bring to a steaming boil.
2. Add spice bag.
3. Immerse apples in the boiling vinegar/syrup solution for 2 minutes.
4. Place apples and spice bag in a crock and add hot syrup.
5. Cover and leave overnight.
6. Remove spice bag, drain syrup into a pan, and bring to a steaming boil.
7. Fill hot pint jars with apples and hot syrup, leaving 1/2-inch of space. Release air bubbles.
8. Close the jars tightly, then heat for 5 minutes in a water bath.

78. Zucchini-pineapple

Ingredients:

- 4 quarts cubed or shredded zucchini
- 46 oz. canned unsweetened pineapple juice
- 1 1/2 cups bottled lemon juice
- 3 cups sugar

Directions:

1. Mix zucchini with other Ingredients in a pan; bring to a steaming boil. Simmer 20 minutes.
2. Fill hot jars with hot mixture and cooking liquid, leaving 1/2-inch of space. Release air bubbles. Close the jars tightly, then heat for 5 minutes in a water bath.

CHAPTER 10: SOUPS AND STOCK

79. Beef Stock

MAKES: 2

Ingredients:

- Beef bones
- Water

Directions:

1. After cracking the beef bones, rinse and place in a stockpot filled with enough water to cover the bones. Heat until boiling. Afterwards, simmer for about three to four hours.
2. Discard the bones and let the broth cool before skimming excess fat. Reheat the broth and then pour into clean and hot Mason jars, each with a one-inch of space remaining.
3. Adjust the lids after removing air bubbles and process in the pressure canner for 20 minutes.

80. Bread and Bean Chard Soup

MAKES: 6-7

Ingredients:

- 2 shallots
- cloves of garlic, chopped
- 1 tablespoon thyme
- 6 slices of bacon
- 100 grams bread, cubed
- 100 grams beans, soaked overnight and drained
- 10 green beans
- 1 Swiss chard, chopped
- 800 ml vegetable soup
- 2 tomatoes, chopped
- 2 tablespoons balsamic vinegar
- 1 bunch of basil
- Salt and Pepper
- Olive oil

Directions:

1. Place the bacon on a baking sheet and fry until crispy at 160 ° C for about 14 minutes.
2. Fry the shallots, garlic, chard, and beans.
3. Pour on the soup and simmer for 10 minutes.
4. Add tomatoes, remaining beans, thyme, salt, pepper, and vinegar.
5. Mix bread with the soup and garnish with basil and bacon.

---

81. Chicken Stock

MAKES: 2

Ingredients:

- Chicken bones
- Water

Directions:

1. Fill a large stockpot with your large chicken or turkey bones. Pour some water into it, enough to cover the bones, then cover and simmer for thirty to forty-five minutes.
2. Discard the bones and let the broth cool before removing excess fat. Reheat before pouring into clean and hot Mason jars, each left with one-inch of space.
3. Adjust the jar lids before processing in the pressure canner for 20 minutes.

CHAPTER 11: KOMBUCHA AND WATER KEFIR

82. Blush rose kombucha

SERVES 4

Ingredients:

- 2 cups diced strawberries, mashed and strained
- 3 cups green tea kombucha
- 2 teaspoons rosewater

Directions:

1. Add the green tea kombucha to the strawberry liquid.
2. Add the rosewater to the jar, stir, and serve over ice.

83. Citrus Kefir

MAKES: 2 cups

Ingredients:

- 2 cups milk kefir.
- 2 to 4 tablespoons citrus juice.

Directions:

1. Blend the citrus juice into the milk kefir and serve.

84. Cocoa Spice Milk Kefir

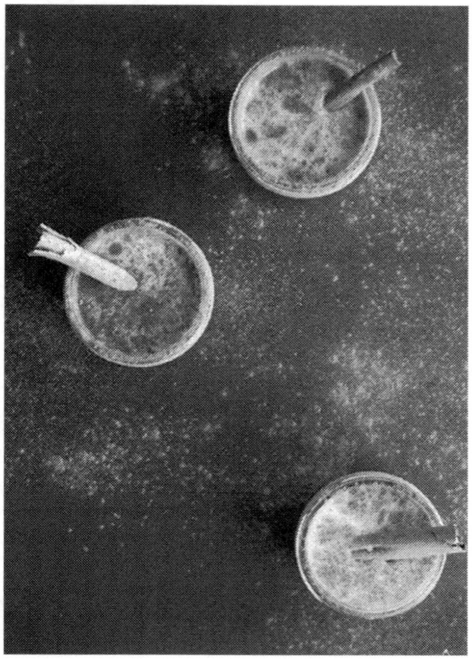

MAKES: 4 cups

Ingredients:

- 4 cups milk kefir.
- 5 tablespoons cocoa powder.
- 2 cloves.
- 2 tablespoons ground cinnamon.
- ¼ tablespoon nutmeg.
- Organic cane sugar or stevia

Directions:

1. Make traditional milk kefir, letting the kefir ferment at room temperature for 24 hours.
2. Strain out the kefir grains and move them to fresh milk.
3. Add the cocoa powder, cloves, cinnamon and nutmeg and stir them into the kefir.
4. Place a lid on the kefir and let it ferment for an addition 12 to 24 hours.
5. Add sweetener.

---

85. Carrot Kefir

MAKES: 2 cups

Ingredients:

- 2 cups milk kefir.
- ½ cup carrot juice.
- ½ cup shredded carrots.
- 1 teaspoon vanilla extract.
- Sweetener
- Fermenting vessel.

Directions:

1. Make traditional milk kefir. The first ferment should last 12 to 24 hours. Strain out the kefir grains before adding any of the other ingredients to the fermenting vessel.
2. Place the milk kefir in the fermenting vessel and add the carrots, carrot juice and vanilla to the container.
3. Place the cover or lid on the container and allow it to ferment for an additional 12 hours.
4. Right before serving, place the kefir in the blender and blend everything together. Add sweetener. Stevia and rapadura are both good choices for sweetener.

86. Ginger kombucha

SERVES 2

Ingredients:

- 1½ cups kombucha, any type
- 1-inch ginger knob, peeled and grated

Directions:

1. Pour the kombucha into a glass.
2. Place the ginger gratings in cheesecloth and squeeze the juice from the gratings into the glass.
3. Stir, pour half of the mixture into a second glass, and serve.

87. Kefir Egg Nog

MAKES: 4 cups

Ingredients:

- 4 cups traditional kefir.
- 2 eggs.
- 2 to 3 tablespoons organic cane sugar.
- ½ teaspoon cinnamon.
- ½ teaspoon nutmeg.

Directions:

1. Combine the kefir, eggs, sugar, cinnamon and nutmeg in a blender and pulse until smooth.
2. Sprinkle a bit of nutmeg mixed with cinnamon on top of each cup as you pour it.

88. Kefir Protein Power Shake

MAKES: 2 cups

Ingredients:

- 1 ½ cups milk kefir.
- 1 – 2 scoops of your favorite protein powder blend.
- ½ cup milk.

Directions:

1. Place all of the ingredients in a big shaker bottle and shake until blended.
2. Drink immediately.

---

89. Kefir Raspberry Flaxseed Fiber Booster

MAKES: 2 cups

Ingredients:

- 2 cups milk kefir
- 2 tablespoons ground flaxseed
- ½ cup raspberries
- Organic cane sugar

Directions:

1. Combine the ingredients mentioned above in a blender and blend them together.
2. Add sweetener if you'd like. Serve.

90. Piña Colada Kefir

MAKES: 2 cups

Ingredients:

- 1 cups milk kefir.
- ½ cup coconut cream.
- ½ cup pineapple juice.
- Blender.

Directions:

1. Place the milk kefir, coconut cream and pineapple juice in the blender.
2. Blend them together.
3. Serve. You can blend ice into the kefir if you want it to be like a smoothie.

91. Strawberry Banana Kefir Smoothie

MAKES: 4 cups

Ingredients:

- 1 cup milk kefir.
- 6 to 8 strawberries.
- 1 banana.
- 5 ice cubes.

Directions:

1. Add the ingredients mentioned above to a blender and blend them together.
2. Serve.

92. Strawberry Lime Kefir Smoothie

MAKES: 4 cups

Ingredients:

- 1 cup milk kefir.
- 2 tablespoons lime juice
- 5 strawberries.
- Organic cane sugar
- 5 ice cubes

Directions:

1. Add all the ingredients mentioned above to a blender and blend it all together.
2. Add sugar.

---

93. Sweet Lavender Milk Kefir

MAKES: 4 cups

Ingredients:

- 4 cups milk kefir.
- 2 tablespoons dried lavender flower heads.
- Organic cane sugar or stevia

Directions:

1. Make traditional milk kefir, letting the kefir ferment at room temperature for 24 hours.
2. Strain out the kefir grains and move them to fresh milk.
3. Stir the lavender flower heads into the milk kefir. Do not add the flower heads while the kefir grains are still in the kefir.
4. Place the lid on the kefir and let it sit at room temperature overnight. The second ferment should last 12 to 24 hours.
5. Strain the kefir to get rid of the flower heads.
6. Add cane sugar or stevia. Stir the sweetener into the kefir.

94. Sweet Raspberry Milk Kefir

MAKES: 2 cups

Ingredients:

- 2 cups milk kefir.
- 3 tablespoons raspberry preserves
- Blender.

Directions:

1. Place the milk kefir and the raspberry preserves in the blender.
2. Blend them together.
3. Serve. You can blend ice into the kefir if you want it to be like a smoothie.

95. Sweet Maple Kefir

MAKES: 2 cups

Ingredients:

- 2 cups traditional milk kefir.
- Organic maple syrup

Directions:

1. Stir the maple syrup into the milk kefir.
2. Taste it and add more syrup if it isn't sweet enough.

96. Vanilla Milk Kefir

MAKES: 2 cups

Ingredients:

- 2 cups milk kefir
- 1 teaspoons vanilla extract

Directions:

1. Stir the vanilla into the milk kefir.
2. Enjoy.

97. Vanilla kombucha

SERVES 4

INGREDIENTS:

- 3 cups kombucha, any type
- 1 teaspoon vanilla extract

Directions:

1. In a large pitcher, add the vanilla to the kombucha, stir until blended.
2. Serve over ice.

98. Watermelon Slush Kefir Smoothie

MAKES: 2 cups

Ingredients:

- 1 cup milk kefir.
- 2 cups seedless watermelon, chopped.
- 10 ice cubes.

Directions:

1. Add the ingredients mentioned above to a blender and blend it all together.
2. Serve.

CHAPTER 12: SAUCES

99. Mango sauce

Ingredients:

- 5 1/2 cups mango purée
- 6 Tablespoons honey
- 4 Tablespoons bottled lemon juice
- 3/4 cup sugar
- 2 1/2 teaspoons ascorbic acid
- 1/8 teaspoons ground cinnamon
- 1/8 teaspoons ground nutmeg

Directions:

1. Purée mango in blender.
2. Mix ingredients in a stockpot and heat with continuous stirring, until the mixture reaches 200°F.
3. Fill hot sauce into jars, leaving 1/4-inch of space.
4. Release air bubbles. Close the jars tightly, then heat for 5 minutes in a water bath.

100. Pickled horseradish delish sauce

Ingredients:

- 2 cups freshly grated horseradish
- 1 cup 5% white vinegar
- 1/2 teaspoons pickling salt
- 1/4 teaspoons powdered ascorbic acid

Directions:

1. Combine Ingredients and ill into sterile jars, leaving 1/4-inch of space.
2. Seal jars tightly.

---

101. Red Sauce With Peppers

Ingredients:

- 2 red and yellow peppers, seeded and diced
- 300 grams extra virgin olive oil
- 1 kg green tomatoes, diced
- 600 grams white wine vinegar
- 1 kg white onions, diced
- 300 grams sugar
- 1 double tomato concentrate tube

Directions:

1. Put everything in a saucepan; add the vinegar, sugar and oil and simmer for 15-20 minutes, then add the entire tube of tomato paste.
2. Simmer for about 3 hours.
3. Cover the jars and turn them upside down so that the vacuum is created.
4. Wrap each jar in a napkin and place in a pot .
5. Cover them with water and boil for 20 minutes.

CONCLUSION

This guide is comprised of a wealth of fresh, evidence-based suggestions for safe home canning and preservation for food and drink This will be an important resource for first-time food canners as well as seasoned canners.

Cooking Conversion Chart

-------------------------- **Meaurement** ------------------------------

Cup	Ounces	Milliliters	Tablespoons
1/16 cup	**1/2** oz	**15** ml	**1** Tbsp
1/8 cup	**1** oz	**30** ml	**3** Tbsp
1/4 cup	**2** oz	**59** ml	**4** Tbsp
1/3 cup	**2.5** oz	**79** ml	**5.5** Tbsp
3/8 cup	**3** oz	**90** ml	**6** Tbsp
1/2 cup	**4** oz	**118** ml	**8** Tbsp
2/3 cup	**5** oz	**158** ml	**11** Tbsp
3/4 cup	**6** oz	**177** ml	**12** Tbsp
1 cup	**8** oz	**240** ml	**16** Tbsp
2 cup	**16** oz	**480** ml	**32** Tbsp
4 cup	**32** oz	**960** ml	**64** Tbsp
5 cup	**40** oz	**1180** ml	**80** Tbsp
6 cup	**48** oz	**1420** ml	**96** Tbsp
8 cup	**64** oz	**1895** ml	**128** Tbsp

--------- Temperature ----------		------------- Weight ---------------	
Fahrenheit	**Celsius**	**Imperial**	**Metric**
100 °F	**37** °C	**1/2** oz	**15** g
150 °F	**65** °C	**1** oz	**29** g
200 °F	**93** °C	**2** oz	**57** g
250 °F	**121** °C	**3** oz	**85** g
300 °F	**150** °C	**4** oz	**113** g
325 °F	**160** °C	**5** oz	**141** g
350 °F	**180** °C	**6** oz	**170** g
375 °F	**190** °C	**8** oz	**227** g
400 °F	**200** °C	**10** oz	**283** g
425 °F	**220** °C	**12** oz	**340** g
450 °F	**230** °C	**13** oz	**369** g
500 °F	**260** °C	**14** oz	**397** g
525 °F	**274** °C	**15** oz	**425** g
550 °F	**288** °C	**1** lb	**453** g

INDEX

A

B

C

D

G

H

I

K

M

N

O

P

Q

R

S

T

V

W

Z

Made in United States
Troutdale, OR
09/09/2023

12766934R00042